DIVERSITY AND COEXISTENCE

FOSTERING ACCEPTANCE IN A DIVERSE AND OPEN SOCIETY

DR. ALI RASHID AL NUAIMI

Archway Publishing books may be ordered through booksellers or by contacting:

Archway Publishing
1663 Liberty Drive
Bloomington, IN 47403
www.archwaypublishing.com
844-669-3957

ISBN: 978-1-6657-3826-2 (sc)
ISBN: 978-1-6657-3827-9 (e)

Library of Congress Control Number: 2023902215

Print information available on the last page.

Archway Publishing rev. date: 04/03/2023

CONTENTS

PREFACE

The acceptance of the other—one who is different in terms of race, language, or faith—has always been among the biggest challenges faced by human societies. Such differences have sparked countless wars and conflicts throughout the world. Man, by nature, feels more comfortable among those who are similar to him and fears those who are different. He usually assumes the latter are a threat, whether in the present or in the future.

Faced with this age-old social phenomenon, modern states and societies currently promote a culture of coexistence, tolerance, and pluralism, and are exerting tremendous efforts toward advancing the thought, theory, and culture of a pluralistic society. However, actual changes in human thought and culture—in values, customs, and traditions—remain limited. Such change is a complex process; it cannot be achieved simply by preaching or promoting change through various communication channels.

After three centuries of renaissance, enlightenment, and modernity, Europe awoke to a racist and fanatic mentality that sparked the Second World War, leaving millions of victims. This war was fueled by a racist nationalist ideology that denied the possibility of coexistence with those who were different or held different opinions; adherents to this ideology spared no effort to eradicate and eliminate its targeted victims in the most barbaric and brutal ways.

Since then, and up to the present moment, human societies and states have sought to promote a culture of tolerance and coexistence with the aim of achieving social peace and countering the fanatic, racist, and religious tendencies that threaten security and destabilize societies. Unfortunately, these efforts have not had the desired impact. Racist crimes continue to occur, and are often even more brutal and impactful than in the past. Many societies and countries still suffer from hatred of the "other"—particularly those who are different in terms of race or faith. The resulting instability, in turn, hinders economic development and prosperity. Many people still dream of living in a society where they might enjoy full coexistence while preserving diversity and difference.

This book presents a new vision for how to achieve coexistence in a diverse society. It seeks first to define the origins of the ideological perspective of this desired model of human coexistence. It then presents the pivotal role of coexistence in the growth and sustainability of societies, states, and civilizations, and concludes by introducing the most realistic model of how coexistence can be achieved among peoples of all types and backgrounds, a model that has been enacted in the United Arab Emirates (UAE). The UAE has made it possible for people of all nationalities, faiths, races, and languages—without exception—to coexist in peace and harmony. This real-life example has made manifest the human dream of active coexistence, presenting us with a method for fulfilling the interests and needs of all without provoking any conflicts, violence, or hatred.

CHAPTER 1

COEXISTENCE AND TOLERANCE: SEMANTICS AND MEANING

COEXISTENCE

The word "coexistence" in Arabic is derived from the word "life," wherein life refers to existence and livelihood. Life in the human context requires that all people exist together in one place, in one society, interacting with one another, exchanging interests, and engaging in different types of relationships based on mutual respect and good neighborliness.

Coexistence takes place among individuals and groups that are, in one way or another, different. These people might be born with different characteristics—whether in terms of language, race, color, faith, creed, or sect—but all agree on the desire to live together; they strive to build a society where they might coexist and share the elements of livelihood, with the existence of each member of society depending on the existence of the other members. This exchange of interests

"

means that each party relies on the contributions of all other parties and no party can live isolated from those who are different or bear different views and opinions. This definition of coexistence applies to individuals, groups, and states, and no one party can take part in coexistence without the participation of the other parties. Coexistence is rather a life practice, a pattern of relationships that involves communication, exchange, and continuous giving, and as such it requires the engagement of all coexisting parties.

Coexistence is a social relationship based on shared interests and a common destiny. Participation in this relationship assumes that everyone is seeking—and must protect—some ultimate interest, and it is thus understood that no single party or group will achieve their interests and objectives if they act in opposition to their partners or infringe their rights. Coexistence is the foundation of society and the state. In the absence of coexistence, the social fabric breaks apart and the state loses its stability, security, and perhaps its very existence.

It stands to reason that coexistence is meant to take place between those who have major or radical differences because those who agree or see themselves as similar tend by default to live together without issues, perhaps not even realizing the ways in which they might differ from others, except when they look at them from a personal perspective. Therefore, the idea of coexistence means that a society is composed of human groups with various cultural and social components that contain layers of differences. These differences might be big or small, fundamental or minimal. People might be adherents of the same faith or hail from the same racial group yet speak different languages or have different cultures, lifestyles, customs, and traditions. In other cases, they might be of the same race yet practice different faiths, or they might adhere to the same faith yet follow different creeds. Only when coexistence is considered a worthy value will all members of society accept living together within a common conceptual framework and coexisting in a way that achieves the public interest and guarantees the stability of the society and state.

Coexistence means accepting diversity while fostering positive relationships among the various social, cultural, and religious groups in society. The concept binds the social and cultural components together and knits them into a stable social structure. Without the idea of coexistence, the social structure remains tense and unstable. This tension will erupt periodically, keeping people constantly on edge as they await the next eruption. If we take a closer look at societies with discrimination and racist crimes, we will find that these crimes reoccur frequently and that the relationships among the various groups in such societies are constantly in a state of tension. That is because the value of coexistence is not instilled within the social culture and has not transformed into a steadfast and stable social tradition.

On the level of international relations, the concept of peaceful coexistence emerged following the death of Joseph Stalin, the leader of the Soviet Union, in 1953. During that new era of its history, the USSR coined the slogan "peaceful coexistence" to express its call to live in peace with nations with different ideologies and political systems. The underlying assumption of this concept was that the hostility between the communist and capitalist spheres of influence would come to an end and that peace would be achieved among the countries of the world. Such coexistence would require mutual respect among proponents of different political systems and economic ideologies and the cessation of hostilities among the adherents of differing ideologies. According to the ideal of peaceful coexistence, countries must not interfere in other countries' affairs because of ideological differences. They must instead accept diversity and difference, thereby creating a healthy environment encouraging cooperation, the exchange of interests, and the highest levels of mutual reliance among countries.

The concept of peaceful coexistence has become one of the fundamentals of international relations and a foremost principle of foreign policy. All countries currently claim to seek peaceful coexistence with their neighbors, regardless of whether they actually commit to and abide by this concept in their foreign policies.

In conclusion, coexistence with diversity and difference is an objective for individuals, societies, and states; it is a goal that is sought by mature individuals, conscious societies, and countries benefiting from wise governance and leadership. However, this goal is not easy to achieve. As such, we find that the societies and states that have succeeded in achieving a reasonable level of coexistence constantly seek to reach higher levels, aiming for harmony. Meanwhile, the states and societies that have not managed to advance further along the path of coexistence continue to suffer from instability and decline in their scale of development and growth.

TOLERANCE

"Tolerance" is often used interchangeably with "coexistence," and many studies confuse the two concepts. However, whereas coexistence is an ethical value that governs relations among human beings, "tolerance" in the Arabic language is derived from the word for forgiveness and is associated with the qualities of being good-hearted, noble, and kind. Tolerance does not mean compromise, submission, or leniency; it represents, rather, the decision to acknowledge other people's rights, respect their existence, and value their diversity. Hence, the value of tolerance does not entail the abnegation or ignorance of someone's beliefs. It refers instead to a person's right to adhere to his or her belief and to accept that other people will adhere to theirs.

Tolerance is a cultural structure that manifests itself in a variety of religious, political, social, cultural, and educational spheres. In modern societies, it is considered of utmost ethical importance to acknowledge and incorporate a multiplicity and diversity of views and lifestyles in the spirit of equality, which gives all people the right to make their own decisions on issues where difference applies.

Thus, the concept of tolerance stems from a context of diversity, sharing, and coexistence, whether between individuals, societies, cultures, or civilizations. It means accepting others regardless of their defects and differences and acknowledging their rights to exist and live in freedom and happiness. Tolerance is the art of living together in society while maintaining a safe distance between general life necessities and the needs of one's private life. The aim of those promoting and practicing tolerance is to guarantee a common life in an atmosphere of difference and diversity and therefore to maintain coexistence and diversity and protect the fundamental values of human existence.

Tolerance does not stand in opposition to variance and variety but instead acknowledges that self-confirmation requires that individuals acknowledge their fellows in terms of both their similarities and their differences.

It is true that coexistence and tolerance share many aspects in common. However, tolerance is an ethical value that governs human relationships. It is part of a diverse cultural system that works within the religious, political, social, cultural, and educational spheres to realize a common objective: to instill in people the ability to accept their fellow human beings, regardless of how different they may be, while maintaining their own values, ethics, and faith.

Tolerance and coexistence both have a noble goal: they constitute the pillars of peaceful coexistence among human beings while preserving diversity.

Tolerance does not mean surrendering one's principles and opinions or abstention from showing or defending them. It means finding a common ground for coexistence and mutual respect with those who have different views and beliefs. Thus, tolerance and coexistence become more attuned to the human vision and more responsive to the need for peaceful cohabitation among humans for a better, safer, and more tolerant world that preserves everyone's rights and lives.

The comprehensive meaning of tolerance in the Arabic language focuses on respecting the "other" and accepting him or her in a welcoming, glad, and generous manner. The English meaning, on the other hand, implies accepting the other in a rather reluctant manner and from a superior position, dealing with the other and his or her existence as an act of sympathy and lowering oneself to tolerate his or her existence. The increasing dominance of the meaning of the English term has narrowed the broader, more inclusive Arabic meanings, leading to the incorporation of the negative connotations implied in the English term into the cultural and social use of the term in Arabic. Therefore, the meaning of tolerance has come to imply an imbalance among the various racial and religious components in a society. These connotations are based on concepts such as majority and minority, indigenous and immigrant, and genuine and secondary. Such a meaning implies that one party allows for the existence and continuity of another party, surrendering to and accepting the other as an act of charity. These meanings are not implied in the Arabic word, but they were imported and incorporated into the Arabic word through mistranslations of the English term "tolerance."

This book will focus on the concept of common living and seeks to shed light on the genuine Arabic semantics of the concept of tolerance in a quest to break free from the negative connotations associated with the English term "tolerance."

CHAPTER 2

ETYMOLOGY OF THE CONCEPT OF COMMON LIVING IN OUR CULTURE

This chapter presents three foundational documents for common living in multiethnic, multireligious, and multicultural societies. These documents describe how diverse societies can achieve stability and develop civilization by adopting the concept of common living. Two of the three documents were written by Prophet Mohammad (PBUH), and the third was written by the second caliph, Omar Ibn Al-Khattab.

These documents are considered among the most important manuscripts ever known in the history of humanity. They instill the concepts of common living with diversity and difference and lay the foundations for the values of tolerance, peace, and human fraternity.

FIRST: THE CHARTER OF AL-MADINAH (THE CONSTITUTION OF AL-MADINAH)

The social value of common living was not a concept that emerged from or followed the establishment of Arabic and Islamic societies. It was rather the foundational concept associated with the establishment of Muslim communities. Prophet Mohammed (PBUH) spent the period of Da'awah (Call towards Islam) in Makkah building the Muslim personality. At that time, he did not have the ability to establish and organize society based on the values found within the Islamic Da'awah. As soon as he arrived in Yathrib and changed its name to Al-Madinah, he announced the establishment of the first civil society based on stability, security, and rule of law, whether customary, conventional, or judicial. Prophet Mohammed started with the Document of Al-Madinah, also called the Charter of Al-Madinah or the Constitution of Al-Madinah. These titles all refer to the same text that Prophet Mohammed (PBUH) issued to establish the first multiethnic, multireligious, and multicultural society in the Arabian Peninsula.

In this founding document for the first Muslim community, we see that the focal idea is the value of common living and cooperation, together with respect for difference and diversity, whether ethnic, religious, or cultural. The Charter of Al-Madinah set forth the rules that govern the relations among those who embrace different faiths (the Jews and the Muslims), among those of different ethnicities (the Aws, the Khazraj, and the tribes), and among those who are culturally different (the Ansar [the helpers] and the Muhajirun [the emigrants]). The Charter of Al-Madinah transformed all these elements into one society that lives together in cooperation and solidarity while preserving diversity and difference.

Muhammad Ibn Ishaq Ibn Yasar Al-Madani (80–151 AH/ 699–769 AD), the author of *Al-Sirah Al-Nabawiyah* (*The Life of the Prophet*), which was later edited by Ibn Hisham and attributed to him, described the Charter of Al-Madinah as follows:

> The Prophet (PBUH) made a prescript between the Muhajirun and the Ansar where he reconciled with the Jews, made a bond with them, and assured them of their faith and money. He prescribed the conditions of their obligations and rights.

The core of the Charter was directed towards making peace with the Jews, reassuring them and accepting their faith and rites in an equal and balanced manner that respected both parties. The Prophet prescribed conditions and reciprocal obligations for both Muslims and Jews.

The Charter is composed of 77 articles, each one of which represents a rule or a pillar of life in a society that is based on common living and respect for difference and diversity. Subsequently, the concept of common living did not become a mere cultural value but rather a core concept governed by law, customs, and contractual rules.

The Charter's introduction provides a definition and etymology of the concept of *Ummah* that incorporates the concept of identity. Prophet Mohammad (PBUH) says,

> This is a document from Muhammad the Prophet (may Allah bless him and grant him peace), governing relations between the Believers (i.e., Muslims) of Quraysh and Yathrib and those who followed them and worked hard with them. They form one nation—Ummah.

The Ummah is not defined as a single entity but as different components and entities, each of which is governed by its own customs and ethnic and cultural ties. Therefore, the idea of Al-Aqilah, emphasized later in Islamic jurisprudence, put forth the theory that determines which groups of people are liable for blood money, outstanding debts, and other financial obligations for their members. The Charter states that the "Muhajirun" are an independent Aqilah from the "Al-Ansar" and that every tribe or independent group of people constitutes an independent Aqilah.

In the following paragraphs of the Charter, it is stated,

> The Quraysh Mohajirun will continue to pay blood money, according to their present customs. In case of war with anybody they will redeem their prisoners with kindness and justice common among Believers. The Bani Awf will decide on the blood money, within themselves, according to their existing customs. In case of war with anybody all parties other than Muslims will redeem their prisoners with kindness and justice according to practice

among Believers and not in accordance with pre-Islamic notions.

This explanation then continues for each tribe and sub-clan of Al-Ansar and defines the Aqilah of each. The Charter also states that the Bani Saeeda, the Bani Harith, the Bani Jusham, the Bani Najjar, the Bani Amr, Bani Awf, Bani Al-Nabeet, and Bani Al-Aws will be governed along the lines of the above principles, until the Prophet Mohammed (PBUH) says, "And the believers shall not leave anyone, hard-pressed with debts, without affording him some relief, in order that the dealings between the believers be in accordance with the principles of goodness and justice." This proves that ideas of cooperation, solidarity, and steadfastness were present among the different social elements, which were able to coexist in peace in a civil society governed by the rule of law provided for in the Charter of Al-Madinah.

Furthermore, the Charter of Al-Madinah introduces the concept of citizenship as known to modern societies and establishes the definition of Ummah as a legal and political boundary for a multireligious, multicultural, and multiethnic society in which social relations are governed by rights and national obligations. It states,

> The Jews of Banu 'Awf shall be considered as one community (Ummat) along with the believers—for the Jews their religion, and for the Muslims theirs, be one client or patron. But whoever does wrong or commits treachery brings evil only on himself and his household.

Then, it enumerates the tribes, families, clients, and supporters of the Jews and details their rights and duties:

> The Jews of Banu-an-Najjar shall have the same rights as the Jews of Banu 'Awf. And the Jews of Banu-al-Harith shall have the same rights as the Jews of Banu 'Awf. And the Jews of Banu Sa'ida shall have the same rights as the Jews of Banu 'Awf. And the Jews of Banu Hisham shall have the same rights as the Jews of Banu 'Awf. And the Jews of Banu al-Aws shall have the same rights as the Jews of Banu 'Awf. And the Jews of Banu Tha'laba shall have the same rights as the Jews of Banu 'Awf. But whoever does wrong or commits treachery brings evil only on himself and his household. And Jafna, who are a branch of the Tha'laba tribe, shall have the same rights as the mother tribes. And Banu-ash-Shutaiba shall have the same rights as the Jews of Banu 'Awf, and they shall be faithful to, and not violators of the treaty. And the mawlas (clients) of Tha'laba shall have the same rights as those of the original members of it. And the sub-branches of the Jewish tribes shall have the same rights as the mother tribes. The Jews who follow our path will be supported, treated equally, and protected.

In the articles above, Prophet Mohammad (PBUH) used the concept of Ummah twice to refer to two distinct, yet interconnected and integrated, meanings. The first instance is when he described Al-Muhajirun and Al-Ansar and their tribes and clans as "a distinct Ummah." In this case, Ummah refers to religious and cultural identity and spiritual bonds. Meanwhile, when the Jews, with their tribes and clans, are mentioned, they are referred to as an "Ummah alongside the Muslims," in other words as an independent spiritual, religious, and cultural group. The concept of Ummah here refers to the national boundary and the concept of citizenship, which gathers people who are religiously, ethnically, and culturally different under the one and only umbrella of the "homeland," where their relations are governed by law. In those times, the law was the Charter of Al-Madinah.

On the other hand, the previous paragraphs highlight the diversity and differences among all of the social elements and faiths. Prophet Mohammad (PBUH) listed all the Muslim tribes in Al-Madinah as well as the Jewish tribes to emphasize the importance and necessity of respecting diversity and difference. He sought to highlight that there must be coexistence among people who come from different religious, ethnic, and cultural backgrounds. Diversity and difference do not hinder peaceful coexistence, but rather affirm it and make it a necessity upon which societies and nations stand and grow. Diversity and difference are the nature of human societies, and the real challenge for these societies is the way they ingrain coexistence into the cultural, legal, and institutional levels and create legal and customary organizational frameworks to govern coexistence and prevent groups from violating or destabilizing it.

The Charter of Al-Madinah further demonstrates the rules of coexistence within an ethnically, religiously, and culturally diverse society. These rules govern economic, social, and political life as well as the foreign relations of the different elements of society that coexist in peace under the rule of law and the organizational frameworks that control and preserve social stability.

The Charter continues listing the rights and obligations of the people of Al-Madinah, stating the following:

> The Jews must bear their own expenses (in War) and the Muslims bear their expenses.

> If anyone attacks anyone who is a party to this Pact the other must come to his help. They (parties to this Pact) must seek mutual advice and consultation. Loyalty gives protection against treachery. Those who avoid mutual consultation do so because of a lack of sincerity and loyalty.

> A man will not be made liable for the misdeeds of his ally. Anyone (any individual or party) who is wronged must be helped. The Jews must pay (for war) with the Muslims. (This clause appears to be for occasions when Jews are not taking part in the war. Clause 37 deals with occasions when

they are taking part in war). Yathrib will be a Sanctuary for the people of this Pact. A stranger (individual) who has been given protection (by anyone party to this Pact) will be treated as his host (who has given him protection) while (he is) doing no harm and is not committing any crime. Those given protection but indulging in anti-state activities will be liable to punishment. A woman will be given protection only with the consent of her family (Guardian). In case of any dispute or controversy, which may result in trouble the matter must be referred to Allah and Muhammed His Prophet (may Allah bless him and grant him peace) who will accept anything in this document, which is for (bringing about) piety and goodness. Quraysh and their allies will not be given protection. The parties to this Pact are bound to help each other in the event of an attack on Yathrib. If they (the parties to the Pact other than the Muslims) are called upon to make and maintain peace (within the State) they must do so. If a similar demand (of making and maintaining peace) is made on the Muslims, it must be carried out, except when the Muslims are already engaged in a war in the Path of Allah.

Everyone (individual) will have his share (of treatment) in accordance with what party he belongs to. Individuals must benefit or suffer for the good or bad deeds of the group they belong to. Without such a rule party affiliations and discipline cannot be maintained. The Jews of al-Aws, including their freedmen, have the same standing, as other parties to the Pact, if they are loyal to the Pact. Loyalty is a protection against treachery. Anyone who acts loyally or otherwise does it for his own good (or loss). Allah approves this Document. This document will not (be employed to) protect one who is unjust or commits a crime (against other parties of the Pact). Whether an individual goes out to fight (in accordance with the terms of this Pact) or remains in his home, he will be safe unless he has committed a crime or is a sinner.

Allah is the Protector of the good people and those who fear Allah, and Muhammad (may Allah bless him and grant him peace) is the Messenger of Allah (He guarantees protection for those who are good and fear Allah).

The Charter of Al-Madinah laid out the practical and realistic foundations of Islamic values and ideas, such as tolerance and coexistence in a pluralistic society. At the time of Islam's foundation, Muslims and Jews from different tribes were living together in Al-Madinah. There were no Christians in Al-Madinah or the surrounding area;

the Christians lived in the north and south of the Arabian Peninsula. Therefore, to demonstrate the principle of social inclusiveness in the time of Prophet Mohammed (PBUH), it was necessary to recall the visit of the Najran Christian delegation from the south of the Arabian Peninsula to the Prophet (PBUH) at Al-Madinah during the year of delegations. The delegations were hosted in the Masjid of the Prophet (PBUH), with the delegation members either holding their crosses or wearing them. In the histories describing this visit, it is never said that the Prophet (PBUH) or any of his companions expressed feelings of discomfort upon seeing these crosses. Furthermore, at prayer time these devout Christians decided to leave the Masjid to perform their prayers. However, the Prophet (PBUH) insisted that they pray inside the Masjid.

The Charter of Al-Madinah and Prophet Mohammed's stance with the Christians of Najran established peaceful coexistence with different religious, racial, and cultural groups as a pillar of the Muslim community and a core element of Islam's vision for society. Through coexistence, a society can achieve stability, safety, and prosperity for all people without exception.

SECOND: THE ASHTINAME OF MOHAMMED WITH SAINT CATHERINE'S MONASTERY

This manuscript has been little researched due to the state of isolation that surrounds Saint Catherine's Monastery on Mount Sinai in Egypt. However, it provides a deeper and more inclusive understanding of the ways in which the values of interfaith tolerance and respect are instilled in Muslims, presenting a practical image, established 1,400 years ago, of how to achieve coexistence with people of different backgrounds. At the time the manuscript was written, people bearing different views or coming from different backgrounds were treated with violence, killing, expulsion, and forced migration.

This manuscript is available in the library at Saint Catherine's Monastery, and Professor Hassan Badawi from the Aristotle University of Thessaloniki has informed me that many copies can be found in neighboring monasteries located in northern Greece on the Holy Mountain in Thessaloniki. He also confirmed that the Ottoman State Archives keep original copies of the manuscript.

The authenticity of this document is reflected in the fact that its terms have been observed by all of the Islamic states that have ruled in the region, from the time of the caliphate to the founding of the modern state of Egypt, from the Umayyad, Abbasid, and Fatimid caliphates to the Ayyubid, Mamluk, and Ottoman sultanates. These dynasties have all preserved and maintained the status of Saint Catherine's Monastery under the control of Greek Orthodox monks. From the time of the Prophet to the current Egyptian government, the monastery has been considered a Greek property, with it being accorded a similar status today as the Greek Embassy. The Egyptian police do not enter the premises of the monastery but provide security around it. The Jabbaliyah Muslim tribe in Sinai, which has had a pact of service and protection with the monks of Saint Catherine for more than 2,000 years, serves the monastery to the present day.

The Promise to St. Catherine's Monastery reads as follows:

> This is a letter which was issued by Mohammed, Ibn Abdullah, the Messenger, the Prophet, the Faithful, who is sent to all the people as a trust on the part of God to all His creatures, that they may have no plea against God hereafter. Verily God is Omnipotent, the Wise. This letter is directed to the embracers of Islam, as a covenant given to the followers of Jesus the Nazarene in the East and West, the far and near, the Arabs and foreigners, the known and the unknown.

> This letter contains the oath given unto them, and he who disobeys that which is therein will be considered a disbeliever and a transgressor to that whereunto he is commanded. He will be regarded as one who has corrupted the oath of God, disbelieved His Testament, rejected His Authority, despised His Religion, and made himself deserving of His Curse, whether he is a Sultan or any other believer of Islam. Whenever Christian monks, devotees and pilgrims gather together, whether in a mountain or valley, or den, or frequented place, or plain, or church, or in houses of worship, verily we are [at the] back of them and shall protect them, and their

properties and their morals, by Myself, by My Friends and by My Assistants, for they are of My Subjects and under My Protection.

I shall exempt them from that which may disturb them; of the burdens which are paid by others as an oath of allegiance. They must not give anything of their income but that which pleases them—they must not be offended, disturbed, coerced, or compelled. Their judges should not be changed or prevented from accomplishing their offices, nor the monks disturbed in exercising their religious order, or the people of seclusion be stopped from dwelling in their cells.

No one is allowed to plunder these Christians, or destroy or spoil any of their churches, or houses of worship, or take any of the things contained within these houses and bring them to the houses of Islam. And he who takes away anything therefrom, will be one who has corrupted the oath of God, and, in truth, disobeyed His Messenger.

Jizya should not be put upon their judges, monks, and those whose occupation is the worship of God; nor is any other thing to be taken from them, whether it be a fine, a tax or any unjust right. Verily I shall keep their compact, wherever they may be, in the sea or on the land, in the East or West, in the North or South, for they are under My Protection and the testament of My Safety, against all things which they abhor.

No taxes or tithes should be received from those who devote themselves to the worship of God in the mountains, or from those who cultivate the Holy Lands. No one has the right to interfere with their affairs, or bring any action against them. Verily this is for aught else and not for them; rather, in the seasons of crops, they should be given a Kadah for each Ardab of wheat (about five bushels and a half) as provision for them, and no one has the right to say to them "this is too much," or ask them to pay any tax.

As to those who possess properties, the wealthy and merchants, the poll-tax to be taken from them must not exceed twelve drachmas a head per year (i.e. about 200 modern day US dollars).

They shall not be imposed upon by anyone to undertake a journey, or to be forced to go to war or to carry arms; for the Muslims have to fight for them. Do no dispute or argue with them, but deal according to the verse recorded in the Quran, to wit: "Do not dispute or argue with the People of the Book but in that which is best" [29:46]. Thus they will live favored and protected from everything which may offend them by the Callers to religion (Islam), wherever they may be and in any place they may dwell.

Should any Christian woman be married to a Muslim, such marriage must not take place except after her consent, and she must not be prevented from going to her church for prayer. Their churches must be honored and they must not be withheld from building churches or repairing convents.

They must not be forced to carry arms or stones; but the Muslims must protect them and defend them against others. It is positively incumbent upon every one of the followers of Islam not to contradict or disobey this oath until the Day of Resurrection and the end of the world.

This covenant was transcribed by Ali bin Abi Talib in the Masjid of the Prophet (PBUH) in the presence of a number of the Prophet's companions serving as witnesses: Abu Bakar bin Abi Qahafah, Umar Ibnul Khattab, Othman Bin Affan, Ali Bin Abi Talib, Abdallah Ibn Massa'ud, Al Abbas Bin Abdul Muttalib, and Al Zubair Ibnul 'Awwam.

THIRD: UMAR'S ASSURANCE OF SAFETY TO THE PEOPLE OF AELIA (JERUSALEM)

This document is different from the previous two. It outlines the terms of the victorious party following a war that has caused severe damage. According to this document, the victors must not impose abusive or humiliating terms on the other party. Instead, they, their people, and the followers of their faith must assume responsibility and ensure permanent rights for the losing party until the end of the world. Thus, the victors would win militarily while the opposing party would benefit on the humane level since they would be accorded rights and privileges that they would not have otherwise enjoyed under Roman rule.

We must read and analyze this document within its historical context. Caliph Umar Ibnul Khattab conquered the city of Aelia, or Jerusalem, in 638 AD after a long and brutal war. In this document, he assured the city's residents that he and the generations to come would protect the Christians, guarantee their rights, and ensure that they were free from the injustice and oppression to which they had been subjected before the arrival of the caliph.

Umar Ibnul Khattab's assurance constitutes a pact of protection for Christian churches and properties. This pact is thought to be one of the most important documents in establishing the concepts of tolerance, coexistence, respect for diversity, and the sanctity of the freedom of belief and the right to practice one's beliefs.

In Umar's assurance, we read the following:

In the name of God, the Merciful, the Compassionate. This is the assurance of safety that the servant of God, Umar, the Commander of the Faithful, has given to the people of Aelia. He has given them an assurance of safety for themselves, for their property, their churches, their crosses, the sick and healthy of the city and all the rituals which belong to their religion. Their churches will not be inhabited by Muslims and will not be destroyed. Neither they, nor the land on which they stand, nor their cross, nor their property will be damaged. They will not be forcibly converted. And Jews will not live in Aelia with them. The people of Jerusalem must pay the taxes like the people of other cities and must expel the Byzantines and the robbers. Those of the people of Jerusalem who want to leave with the Byzantines, take their property and abandon their churches and crosses will be safe until they reach their place of refuge. The villagers [who had taken refuge in the city at the time of the conquest] may remain in the city if they wish but must pay taxes like the citizens. Those who wish may go with the Byzantines and those who wish may return to their families. Nothing is to be taken from them before their harvest is reaped. If they pay their taxes according to their obligations, then the conditions laid out in this letter are under

the covenant of God, are the responsibility of
His Prophet, of the caliphs and of the faithful.
Witnessed by: Khalid Ibnul Walid, Amro Ibnul
A's, Abdul Rahman Ibn 'Awf, and Mu'awiyah
Ibn Abi Sufiyan in the 15th year of Al-Hijrah.

The three documents presented here constitute the ideological foundations for the ways Muslim communities have
coexisted with diversity and difference over the past 1,400
years, revealing that such ideas were actually drawn from the
basic rules, fundamentals, and values of Islam.

Coexistence, tolerance, peace, and human fraternity can
be fully realized in Muslim communities by incorporating
the values and principles outlined in the three documents
into attempts to develop community awareness about relations
with non-Muslims. The methods used to establish coexistence within small yet diverse communities can be applied
on a global scale, especially in this era of modern media and
fast communications and knowledge transfer, which will help
the methods to be shared widely. This will allow for success
stories to be shared and learned from around the world.

There is thus an urgent need to revive these values and en-
act them within our societies, transforming them from theory
found in books to the foundations for human behavior. In so
doing, we can introduce the world to successful, attractive examples of coexistence with diversity and difference, examples
that realize people's common interests while preserving their
particularities and identities, without requiring the surrender
of any component of their cultures or beliefs.

CHAPTER 3

COEXISTENCE AND CIVILIZATION BUILDING

When studying both ancient and modern history, one notices that the societies that made remarkable civilizational achievements could have never succeeded without establishing coexistence between people from different cultural, ethnic, and religious backgrounds. Islamic civilization, regardless of its location in the world, was the outcome of interactions among cultural and religious elements that were ethnically, linguistically, and spiritually diverse. Indeed, the first generations of Muslims were aware that the only way to build a civilization suitable for settlement and achieve human happiness was by valuing open-mindedness and coexistence and being willing to take advantage of human capabilities regardless of religious, ethnic, cultural, or linguistic differences.

For more than 800 years during the Rashidun and Umayyad caliphates, Islamic institutions were run and managed by non-Muslim and non-Arab cadres, and the official languages in the state offices were Syriac and Farsi. This continued until the 84th year of Al-Hijrah, when Umayyad Caliph Abdul Malik Ibn Marwan decided to make Arabic the official language of the government.

In addition, the great civilizational revolution during the Abbasid Caliphate was born out of the state's openness to the world, willingness to learn from previous civilizations, and establishment of a pluralist, diverse society that encouraged active interactions among communities of different backgrounds. This era was characterized by the emergence of Arabic translations of the heritage of previous civilizations, such as the Greeks. The pioneers of this movement were Christian, Syriac, and Jewish translators. In some instances, the process involved translation from Greek to Syriac, and then to Arabic.

This beautiful image of coexistence between the different religious, ethnic, and cultural groups was the reason for the success and prosperity of Islamic civilization during the Abbasid era. This success lives on in the present in the fields of biology and mathematics, which the Arabs learned from the works of previous civilizations and built upon, making huge leaps in scientific and mathematical understanding. This knowledge was later taken to Europe, where it was developed further, to the benefit of our world today, in medicine, engineering, technology, and many other scientific fields.

The Islamic civilization in Andalusia provides the clearest illustration of the importance of coexistence with diversity to civilization building and national prosperity. Andalusia was a center of knowledge and education and a bridge for knowledge transfer, with Muslims bringing knowledge originating in the Greek, Indian, and Chinese traditions to Europe. The educational process took place in an open, diverse, and pluralistic environment. The Muslim Arab scientists versed in the various scientific disciplines would deliver their lessons in Arabic. However, since most of the European students spoke Latin rather than Arabic, there was a need for translators from Arabic to Latin. This was the role of the Jews, who mastered both Arabic and Latin. As a result, the classes and sessions that took place in the mosques gathered together Muslim scientists, Christian students, and Jewish translators hailing from countries all around the Mediterranean, speaking Arabic, Latin, and Hebrew.

However, after the expulsion of Muslims and Jews from Andalusia, this beautiful model fell apart. The entire area—which had been enlightened with knowledge for many centuries—was thereafter filled with darkness until the Europeans began to understand the importance of openness, the existence of difference and diversity, and the ways of achieving coexistence to ensure the common good.

Scottish historian and orientalist Hamilton Gibb has a vision that is worthy of consideration. He argues that the Muslims' golden era was the fruit of a cultural alliance between them and the Jews, and that this alliance created a unique example of coexistence in Andalusia and elsewhere. In his analysis, the civilization in Andalusia fell apart as soon as the state of coexistence collapsed, and European civilization evolved because it adopted the same model of coexistence between the Jews and Christians.

Researchers of American history also agree that the Industrial Revolution was fueled by the intellect and labor of immigrants. Henry Ford, the founder of Ford Motors, was the first to recruit manpower from Yemen and Syria for his factories in Detroit, Michigan, to the point that Arab influence became noticeable in the city.

This also applies to the scientific revolution in universities and innovation and research centers. Technological development was heightened following the waves of immigration from Germany and Scandinavia after the First World War, and further advanced with the arrival of talented Jewish experts from all over Europe. The American government still grants US citizenship annually to 50,000 immigrants who are recruited and selected in a deliberate fashion, using contests to select this precise number of candidates regardless of how many applicants the country receives from the four corners of the globe.

The American model of civilization is the most successful example, after the Abbasid Caliphate model, of a society that evolved out of pluralism, diversity, and coexistence and not based on any one race or faith. It also stands as inarguable historical evidence for the value of these ideals.

Another example of growth and prosperity from history is Egypt during the nineteenth and first half of the twentieth century. Egypt hosted immigrants from various Mediterranean countries, especially from the Levant, Greece, Italy, and Tunisia, and the country's cultural, scientific, and arts sectors flourished due to these immigrants' contributions. Those immigrants became more Egyptian than the native Egyptians. The first Egyptian newspaper, *Al-Ahram*, was founded by Beshara and Saleem Takla, two Christian brothers who had moved to Egypt from Syria in 1875. The famous publishing house Dar Al Ma'aref, the first Arab publisher and the third publishing house in the world, was established by the Christian Armenian immigrant Naguib Metri, who came to Egypt in 1890. The contributions of immigrants to Egypt's prosperity encompassed all sectors, including industry, arts, moviemaking, management, administration, and politics. The first prime minister in the history of modern Egypt was Nubar Basha, an immigrant from Armenia, who rose to office in 1879. Moreover, the pioneers of Egyptian popular poetry were Bayram Al-Tunsi, a Tunisian, and Fuad Haddad, whose family was originally from Lebanon.

Egypt progressed thanks to its openness, diversity, and pluralism, and because it ingrained the principle of peaceful coexistence in society. Unfortunately, this model fell apart after the implementation of the nationalization policy and the expulsion of Greek, Italian, and Jewish immigrants following the 1952 revolution.

From these examples, one can see that it is not possible to build a civilization without ingraining the principle of coexistence in the people. A civilization that is capable of self-development and continuous creativity can only grow out of religious, ethnic, and cultural pluralism, and maintaining this kind of civilizational model requires coexistence and tolerance.

The United Arab Emirates has taken this path, following the Egyptian model in building progress and prosperity. When we consider the history outlined in these chapters, it becomes clear that maintaining the UAE's success requires extensive cultural interactions with people from all over the world, through efforts to host the best international ambassadors and attract the most brilliant minds and experts.

CHAPTER 4

THE UAE MODEL: THE POST-COEXISTENCE SOCIETY

The United Arab Emirates is a young country with a rich heritage and deep roots in history. In only 50 years of existence, it has managed to incorporate a cultural and social heritage of more than 2,000 years into a model for sustainable coexistence for inhabitants originating from more than 200 countries. Observers have agreed that the UAE has put forth a successful, durable model that has become an icon of coexistence among peoples of different faiths, races, cultures, and languages. The UAE's diverse residents live together, meet in public spaces in peace and happiness, enjoy this atmosphere, and long to preserve it for generations to come.

Throughout these 50 years of history, the UAE has never recorded a single racist crime. In addition, there is no sort of xenophobia directed toward people of different religious, racial, or linguistic backgrounds. The residents live in peace and harmony, abide by the law, and believe in the rule of law and equality. They also engage in their livelihoods, strive to serve their society, and work to build an example of sustainable development for the happiness and wellbeing of all.

The UAE's history from both ancient and modern times shows that coexistence and tolerance are deeply embedded in the culture of its generous people. The people of the UAE are unique in the extent to which they value these principles, and this state of affairs leads visitors and residents alike to make beautiful memories of their time living in the country. Coexistence is the core cultural element of this country, which has been open to the world since its foundation. The country has been the meeting point of civilizations and cultures and a bridge for trade and the exchange of interests. It has always welcomed strangers regardless of their professed faith or identity. Therefore, the superpowers that controlled the Indian Ocean were assured of a safe house in the UAE, and the first ports and harbors in the region were built on UAE territories. This country has also served as the starting point for many traders traveling to South Asia, Southeast Asia, and Eastern and Southern Africa. The traders spread Islam and their cultures throughout these regions. These influences still exist today in these regions, which are considered among the most peaceful, quiet, and tolerant in the world.

The Emirati model of coexistence with diversity gains more importance in light of increasing human mobility and the emergence of multicultural communities that are not limited by a given inherited culture. Multicultural interaction has become one of the main characteristics of emerging and advanced societies, and economic, scientific, and technological developments have become dependent on social openness, diversity, and pluralism. Adherence to such principles makes it possible for people from different religious, ethnic, and language backgrounds to know one another, interact culturally, and live and work together toward the achievement of one single objective.

At the same time, the definition of tolerance has narrowed due to the influence of Western societies, which equate the concept with mere acceptance—sometimes reluctance—of the other. However, true tolerance requires more than simply accepting those who are different. In a truly tolerant society, the self and the other become interdependent, such that neither party can continue to exist and prosper without the other. Interfaith and intercultural dialogue becomes irrelevant in a truly tolerant society, as such a society has surpassed the need for such dialogue.

True tolerance allows all members of society to embrace their practices in total freedom, allowing them to interact socially and work toward the public interest alongside their fellows regardless of faith and culture. In this way, societies can achieve real progress and prosperity, carving out a better future for future generations. Active coexistence has thus become a framework that preserves cultural uniqueness for all while benefiting society. By following the path of true tolerance and coexistence that the UAE has laid out, other countries can broaden their understanding of such concepts and approach the world from a fair and humane perspective, without feelings of superiority or inferiority.

Given the UAE's technical structure, which supports coexistence, tolerance, and understanding, the country's residents possess a unique vision on matters of global importance. They are able to understand the challenges faced by countries and communities worldwide and show these communities a way forward that will benefit all.

The UAE is much like an experimental laboratory for the future of humanity. Its experiences prove to the world that peace and true tolerance can be achieved in human societies and that coexistence amidst diversity is a reality. The only elements required to achieve this reality are the rule of law, the application of a fair justice system, and the common desire that all people are able to lead a happy and prosperous life. These conditions create a favorable environment for people to spread kindness and eliminate hatred, racism, and extremism.

Purposeful and careful attention from the UAE's leadership has led tolerance and coexistence to become the country's social and cultural reality. The leadership is aware that passing on this consciousness to future generations will require new tools. As such, the Ministry of Tolerance and Coexistence was established to ensure that these values are carried forward. This wise decision will institutionalize the UAE's model for tolerance and coexistence.

The United Arab Emirates can serve as a leading global center for all those who wish to discuss and learn about ways to build societies that adopt and embody a culture of coexistence. In this way, the UAE could guide countries towards peace and prosperity and away from conflict, war, and destruction. The UAE has several strengths that enable it to act as such a light in the world:

- The UAE has a beneficial geographic location and regional and global status. This is particularly true with regard to the special status and role of the country's founding father, Sheikh Zayed Bin Sultan Al Nahyan (May Allah rest his soul in peace). This status is embodied in the country's pride in its Arab and Islamic heritage and in its achievements in all sectors, especially in the ways it has ingrained the values of religious tolerance and understanding into the country's progress and prosperity at the local, regional, and global levels.

- The UAE's leadership is keen to make the country a beacon of moderate and enlightened thought that is open to the entire world.

- The UAE has global ties and is attractive to people from all around the world, who are eager to travel to the country and reside there. This has made the UAE a global center for civilization, a space for intercultural interaction and cooperation, and an example of enlightened thought that serves all of humanity.

- The UAE has seen remarkable cross-sector developments and achievements, and the leadership has fostered a humane and harmonious environment that has been free from racist crimes and sectarian acts since the country's establishment.

- The rule of law, which established a fair legal system that makes no exceptions and affords no privileges, ensures that all people are equal before the law. This legal system remains in step with social changes and grants coexistence and tolerance a legal status that is protected by law. In this context, the UAE passed the Anti-Hatred and Anti-Discrimination Law in 2015, and later the Civil Law for Non-Muslims. These laws assured everyone living in the country of their right to coexist while preserving their differences, thus high-lighting diversity as a vital feature of a humane society and an important source of intellectual richness.

The United Arab Emirates succeeded in instilling tolerance as an ingrained element of the social fabric. Tolerance was then made part of the public order, protected and preserved by law. The state further established regulations and institutions designed to promote and ingrain tolerance in the social consciousness, so that future generations would also be able to walk the path of their ancestors, who were tolerant by nature and had tolerance embedded within the core of their traditions. It was finally able to introduce the world to a model of a post-tolerance society, presenting an active, sustainable model for coexistence that guarantees the continuity of religious, ethnic, and cultural diversity and difference, and indeed, considers these to be a vital source of community and national richness. Within this diverse, pluralistic society, all peoples coexist and work towards the welfare of all. This is how nations are built and the future is made—a future that promises to provide security and happiness to the entire human race.

CONCLUSION

HOW CAN THE WORLD LIVE AND COEXIST WITH DIVERSITY AND DIFFERENCE?

All processes of social and cultural change begin with education. New values must first be ingrained in people's hearts the values and then be enshrined and protected in law. Laws become thus the fortress that surrounds and protects society and its institutions, values, and traditions from trespassers who, driven by illusive and misleading inclinations, hate the stability provided by social rules.

However, when it comes to ingraining coexistence and tolerance within the cultural fabric of diverse and pluralistic societies, the change cannot end with better education and laws. The following steps address the question, "How can the world live and coexist with diversity and difference?" These steps provide a roadmap for a future in which the higher values of life are prized and honored.

- The countries of the world should issue laws and regulations to eradicate terrorism and extremism. States and societies achieve success, stability, and continuity with the rule of law, not simply through persuasion and kindness. The rule of law is the way that keeps people away from being subject to the law. In order to establish rule of law, some countries will need to reform their educational systems and religious discourse. As mentioned above, in 2015 the United Arab Emirates became the first country to pass the Anti-Hatred and Anti-Discrimination Law. This step placed the UAE at the forefront of countries that respect pluralism and coexistence and led to the country becoming a center for investment, tourism, and many other economic and cultural activities. Unfortunately, no other country has issued a law criminalizing hatred, discrimination, and racism, under the pretext of freedom of opinion and expression. International events and incidents over the last 20 years have proven that such freedoms are nothing more than political tools. Countries that position themselves as the guardians of freedom wield these tools to achieve their own aims and interests. But when this freedom conflicts with their interests, such as when people use this freedom to voice opposing opinions, these countries are quick to sacrifice their principles and restrain the freedom they once lauded. This is done under various pretexts and using the seemingly inexhaustible supply of mottos and slogans put forth by those in control of international organizations.

- A global reform of the education system led by the United Nations Educational, Scientific, and Cultural Organization (UNESCO) and aimed at removing from the formal curriculum or extracurricular activities any content that stands to incite hatred, discrimination, or racism. Education should focus on ingraining coexistence, tolerance, and respect for diversity into the cultural fabric. There should be a global educational observatory that tracks curricula from all over the world, identifies any breaches or violations, and reports them to UNESCO, which would take necessary actions in accordance with the regulations of the UN.

- The arts are crucial in the formation of a common collective awareness. It is necessary to formulate a global charter to combat hatred, racism, and discriminatory discourse and to make theater, film, and all other forms of art free from ideas that incite racism or contempt for the other. In addition, there should be a global award for artworks that encourage and promote coexistence, tolerance, and respect. The largest global film festivals and award shows, such as those in Cannes and Hollywood, should also dedicate a special award for films that promote these values.

- There must be strict controls on social media platforms to criminalize discourse inciting hatred and racism. Such posts and comments should be banned, and accounts that publish them should be blocked. This can be controlled by adjusting algorithms on each social media platform with the support of their advisory committees. It is also necessary to have legal controls in place to handle the non-compliance of social media platforms.

- There should be a global journalism charter that criminalizes faith-based aggression, respects diversity and difference, and combats discrimination and hateful discourse. The freedom of the press must not be a tool for inciting racism, discrimination, and hatred of others. Furthermore, the charter must be adopted by the General Assembly of the United Nations, and all countries must commit to the charter by enshrining it in their national laws.

- A conference of global religious leaders should convene and agree upon a charter of religious freedom. This would be in the same spirit as the Document on Human Fraternity, which was signed by Pope Francis of the Catholic Church and the Sheikh of Al-Azhar in Abu Dhabi in 2019. This document should state that discriminatory discourse and faith-based hatred and criticism must be banned in keeping with the Quranic verse, "You shall have your religion and I shall have my religion."

If these six conditions were fulfilled, worldwide populations could coexist and live peacefully in religiously, ethnically, and culturally diverse communities and societies, and our children and grandchildren would grow up in a safer, happier, and more stable world. The United Arab Emirates has provided a model that proves that this is not a mere dream. It would be easy to achieve this model on a global scale if all countries would carefully study and implement the conditions necessary to transform this dream into a reality.

www.ingramcontent.com/pod-product-compliance
Lightning Source LLC
Chambersburg PA
CBHW051418250726
48655CB00003B/1123